How to Rank and Prioritize Nearly Anything

Team Decision Matrix

Parag Vaish

Contents

Introduction   1

Chapter: 1 The Problem with Prioritization   13

Chapter: 2 Rank and Prioritize Anything with this Model   41

Chapter: 3 Always Keep Context in Mind   77

Chapter: 4 Other uses of prioritization and rank model   83

Conclusion   89

Dedicated to the following people for their continued unconditional support:

Vivek Bhaskaran, Bill Furlong, George Grobar, Jeremy Holland, Chandra Khattak, Gautam Khattak, Veena Khattak, Dean Lyettefi, Boyd Mark, Paul Maya, Mats Nilsson, Ambar Pansari, Mario Ribera, Chris Tsakalakis, Aparna Singhal, Chandre Sarkar Singhal, Nikhyl Singhal, Nithin Singhal, Ravi Singhal, Vivek Singhal, Ram Srinivasan, Gita Vaish, Harish Vaish, Nalin Vaish, Payal Khattak Vaish, Saanya Savitri Vaish, Eric Vasquez, Brant Williams and Arthur Kah-Git Wong.

Introduction

My name is Parag Vaish, and in this book, you'll learn about a methodology to rank and prioritize nearly anything. This model, which I call the Team Decision Matrix model, has been years in the making and I've perfected it through my experience as an individual who has had the privilege of working with many great companies. These companies are in vastly different industries from one another, which gives me confidence that this model will work in almost any environment. The collective wisdom I've gained while working with these companies has fueled my understanding of how the decision-making process works; all of which has led to the creation of this book.

To give you a bit of context, I started out my career working for The Walt Disney Company as a senior financial analyst in the live-action film division. This was the division which made movies such as; *Enemy of the State, The Sixth Sense, Armageddon, Pirates of the Caribbean,* and *Pearl Harbor,* to name a few. I was tasked with projecting profit and loss for feature films, in all media formats, and all markets around the world. My job involved gathering enough information to reflect a picture of the film's financial health before any film was shot. This was often two or three years before the movie would release in theaters. Think about that for a moment: "What was the probable financial outcome in all media formats globally of an action thriller starring Will Smith with a $100M production budget?" To start to answer this question, I looked at the filmography of each of the main actors, or the lead supporting actors, of the film in question to see all past performance tendencies of those actors. Following this, I would look at the recent past performance history of movies in a similar genre. If it was a romance film, then I would check how other romance films tended to do across different markets around the world. Lastly, I would analyze how much revenue was earned on movies that had a similar budget size. All of these data points resulted in a picture of how the movie was possibly going to do based on all these vectors. I had no idea that what I was learning in 1997 would be something I would refer to nearly a decade later, which was the catalyst for the Team Decision Matrix model.

While working as a financial analyst, I had to deal with incredible uncertainty and any analysis I provided could result in Disney losing a lot of money. You can see how that might lead to a lot of stress. However, I've always believed in the power of data, and, if you have data to back up your decisions, then you're less likely to make bad ones. My role at Disney allowed me to start developing the skill of getting data, where data isn't typically available, and proceeding forward in high stakes situations. It was this foundation which laid the groundwork for a different application of the same logic: about 15 years later.

I'm genuinely passionate about this model, and I absolutely believe in its power to help anyone rank and prioritize nearly anything. This model will not only help you make informed decisions, but it will also help all the other people involved feel like their opinions are being heard and respected. I'm excited to be sharing it here with you in detail.

I've developed the Team Decision Matrix model by executing the tenets of my trade, which has generally been in the area of product management discipline, an area where decision-making played a key part of the role. Therefore, its foundations were built on the experiences that I had while working for places like Microsoft, Escapia (bought by HomeAway), NBC, athenahealth, StubHub, and Tesla. And, as of the time publishing this book, I will have just joined Google. All these companies vary in terms of industry - from filmmaking to media, travel, healthcare, energy, and automotive industries. Working at companies in various industries has taught me is that the core principles of product management stay the same regardless of the industry focus. You can generally apply the same decision-making process across any industry if you understand the essence of what it means to make smart decisions.

As I worked with these companies over the years, I came to realize that there were similar challenges within these companies that led them to make less than desirable decisions. One of the major problems I noticed across the board is a lack of proven data that can back up decisions being made - making it hard to justify current actions. This got me thinking about ways we could make decisions based off information and resources that were readily available to anyone - no matter the company or industry. I concluded that a company's most significant resource is its people. This is a bit of knowledge most people are aware of but don't know how to harness or scale in any systematic way. At the same time, I also started thinking about how to create one universal prioritization method that could keep a team focused on producing excellent quality work in a way that made the most of their time, collective knowledge, and each team member's individual respective industry experience. Thus, the Team Decision Matrix model was born.

The Team Decision Matrix model really started shaping into real-life practice in February 2013 during my time at StubHub. I started working at StubHub on February 22nd. The reason that exact date is important is because it was a little more than halfway through the first quarter of the year. What typically starts to happen around that time of year is people start looking at the Q2 roadmap for that year. By the time I got ramped up, it was practically Q2, so we needed to have a clear picture of what we would do in Q2. Corporate America doesn't really give you a pass on a quarter's goals or plans, even if you just started at a company, so my primary question was, "What was the Q2 roadmap?" When I turned to the product managers on my team and asked them about the Q2 roadmap, they gave me a list of eight items. I then asked them where the eight items came from and why were they important. One product manager on my team said, "Well, the first one came from the business development team, the second one came from customer service, the third one's an API that's been discontinued by engineering, the fourth one is from the marketing team," and so forth. What I quickly realized, as this product manager went through the list, is that he was just a recipient of all of these items from different teams in the company. It was just a list. Presumably, a business person wrote in an inquiry that said, "Hey, I'd really like for the StubHub mobile app to have X capability because we have this partner who wants it," and that's how the item got on the list.

Alarmingly, what I found was nothing on that list was rooted in value or impact. Nowhere was item number nine, which didn't make the list, evaluated for its merits relative to the eight that did make the list. It was a very tough roadmap discussion for me because it appeared to me that we, as a product management team, were just taking orders. I looked at this product manager and asked, "What are the names of the people I need to go talk to about these eight projects?" He replied, "I'm sorry, I don't actually know the names of the people who submitted them." Now, there I was in a situation where I've been at the company for about one month, we needed to come up with a Q2 roadmap (considering Q2 was about a week or two away), and I didn't even know who to talk to about these eight projects and discuss the merits and value of each project. All I knew was that somebody somewhere submitted them somehow, and my product manager had taken them and turned the information into a roadmap. What followed was probably one of the bolder moves of my career: I told him that I was going to cancel all of these projects. We were going to make this a blank slate of a roadmap, and I was going to let these eight people come to my desk and tell me why we should pursue these projects. Guess what?! No one showed up. Not a single person came to me to ask what happened to their project, nor to tell me why their project should be pursued.

It was a very fascinating exercise, and that experience served a valuable purpose. I then started asking new questions – "What are all the things we've ever dreamed of, wondered about, thought we should do, had seen our competitors do, etc.?" I ended up with my product managers giving me one hundred ideas/features that encompassed all these attributes. That's why I came up with this model. It was born out of necessity, and frankly, out of a form of crisis. I had one week to create a roadmap, and I had nothing on the roadmap. I didn't really have enough tenure at the company to arbitrarily decide what should be on the roadmap, so how could I create it in a way that I could stand in front of the company and defend the merits of the roadmap?

I thought, "If I were the CEO of a publicly-traded company like eBay (which at the time of printing this book is the owner of StubHub), my goal would be to increase shareholder value." That's it, and usually this is the charter of every CEO of a publicly traded company. But it's tough to turn that into a product roadmap and say, "Feature #22 will increase shareholder value." The gap between the impact of the feature and how the market assesses an increased shareholder value is just too broad. I then looked at which things move the needle on shareholder value and what I came up with was: increased profit, increased revenue, and increased market share. Those three things are the influencers behind increasing shareholder value, in my opinion. To be fair, there may be others, but this is what I decided at the time. Then I looked for which things influence those three values, and that's how I landed on the eventual vectors that I chose, which included increased conversion, increased net promoter score, increased traffic, decreased cost, and increased inventory. Keep in mind, these are specific to StubHub, but can be applied to other e-commerce sites. I then told my product managers that if any of the projects on the list (the features) impact these five vectors in a small, medium, large, or no-impact way then indicate it and we'll be able to get to something that resembles an indication of value. This was all happening quite organically, so I didn't quite think about all this with the result being a scalable decision matrix which would be a key weapon in my arsenal as a product leader - and something I'd ultimately turn into a book.

Decisions that are made without gathering any data are more like a shot in the dark that may or may not reach the intended target. In fact, most projects are likely to fail, on the order of 75% of the time. That's an incredible amount of wasted time and effort. Wouldn't it be better to prioritize specific projects or decisions using a stable foundation of data from individuals who could contribute valuable opinions to the outcome? That's what my model succeeds in doing - it helps people base decisions on quantifiable data and then helps them decide which decision is the best for their respective needs. What's more, this model allows for these decisions to be made with the input from other individuals in a way that gives everyone's input equal weight. I will go into a detailed discussion about the exact inner-workings of the Team Decision Matrix model in the second chapter of this book.

The later chapters in this book will help you use this model effectively and will be a detailed guide on how this model works. But if you're looking for some outside help even after reading this book, then you can head on over to Ideascale. com. I sold the methodology that's been outlined in this book to that company, and they created a product from it called Reviewscale. It's a web-based tool that anyone can use. It will make the execution of the prioritization process easier since all of the structure of the methodology is built into the software, along with tutorials on how to use it. All you then need to do is to fill in the details so you can adapt the model to your specific needs. But that's just a convenient way of going about this. You can still follow all of the steps outlined in this book and use any spreadsheet or data-entry software you prefer to get the same results.

While my model will no doubt be effective for product managers - in particular, those within the field of software development as this is the context I've developed it in - the model isn't just for those that hold managerial positions in software development. It can be implemented by just about anyone in any position or situation, given that the person must prioritize among a long list of options.

I want this book to offer you some helpful advice and information that you can take away and use in everyday life. Whether we actively think about it or not, we're all decision-makers in every aspect of our daily lives. And while the Team Decision Matrix model might not be applicable to all decisions, I hope its core principles can help give structure to your choices where it might have been missing. Through my model, you'll be able to rank and prioritize any difficult decisions that might come your way in the future, whether they are of a professional or personal nature.

Chapter 1

THE PROBLEM WITH PRIORITIZATION

People have to make decisions every day. Some are hard, and others aren't, but they all require a level of prioritization - choosing one thing over another. We choose to go to work instead of staying home, or we choose to attend a meeting instead of gossiping around the water cooler. These aren't hard choices to make. You choose to go to work, for instance, because you prioritize it as an important step towards financial independence. The prioritization process can be classified as a structured approach towards decision-making. The execution order of certain tasks is based on certain per-approved parameters, to ensure the highest efficiency.

However, some choices require a lot more forethought and examination - especially for managers who need to make sure their staff and projects are running smoothly, or for managers who need to choose a new project. Choosing a new project is a major undertaking and can lead to a lot of stress for managers and other staff. Frequently, the ultimate objective, i.e., to gain a certain number of new customers or website traffic, has already been identified. However, the problems usually arise when it comes to choosing the project through which that goal will be reached.

This is why prioritization is critical. You can have the best, most hard-working team, and a good execution plan, but all of that won't mean much if the project they're working on doesn't hold the most value for the company. According to the Project Management Institute, in 2016, for every $1 billion invested in the United States, $122 million was wasted due to lacking project performance. (2016. The High Cost of Low Performance. *Pulse of the Profession, Global Project Management Survey*, 8th ed., p.5)

So, arguably, the most critical part of any manager's job is to dedicate time and energy toward helping others work on projects that will benefit the company. What gives a project value will differ from one company to another, but some general values include, increasing website traffic, higher employee retention, increasing market share, decreasing customer complaints, and so on.

Many factors can hamper the prioritization process. I have outlined some of them below, so you can get a feel for what issues you may be seeing in your own organization. Of course, the issues listed below aren't the end-all be-all of the problems with prioritization. Each company and each situation is unique, so the point of this list is to show how important prioritization is and how often proper prioritization can be neglected.

Prioritization isn't being prioritized

People often dedicate a lot of time towards tasks and projects but rarely make sure to set aside enough time for prioritization. Mostly, this is because people like seeing their work have a visible effect - they like ticking off boxes. Therefore, the process of prioritization can feel like wasted effort to those people. This happens largely because there is no tangible result received in the process and, hence, no immediate gratifying box to tick when they're done. Prioritization is an ongoing process that should be present throughout all stages of product management, and it can even be helpful in some other departments, like human resources. You'll get why I say that when I start discussing my model later in this book.

The point is, if no one takes the time to prioritize goals and tasks effectively, then the chances of everyone's random efforts resulting in a success for the company is slim to none. Without proper prioritization, you're essentially flying blind. So, prioritization should always be a manager's first priority. Still, that doesn't solve the issue of how to effectively prioritize. That's why the Team Decision Matrix model, and this book, exists.

Ideas are cheap

You'll frequently hear a big collective sigh whenever someone mentions the word "brainstorm." Usually, because people feel it's a tedious exercise where their ideas aren't truly being heard. Plus, brainstorming can be taxing on both employees and company time, with no true valuable ideas being put forward. Or at least, the most valuable ones aren't being identified and are, thus, ignored.

Whenever I work with a team, I find that there's usually no

shortage of ideas floating around. People love having their ideas and opinions heard, and there's often information behind each idea. However, not all ideas are equally made, and no two ideas have the same value. The hard part comes when you have to sort the valuable ideas from the less valuable ones.

Here are some facts about the ideation process that I've come across in my work:

- Ideas don't always consider what can actually be executed in a relevant timespan

- Ideas are often void of the value or cost

- Ideas are usually formed with one viewpoint in mind, instead of a more all-encompassing perspective (think: sample size of one person)

- Some people are too afraid to give their input, which results in the loss of their unique perspective

- People sometimes refuse to adapt their views when presented with new information, because they are wedded to "their" idea

While it's great that ideas are being generated for new

projects, the more important part of the process is to ensure that the right ideas are prioritized so the project can align with the company's vision. One of the biggest challenges for managers is to balance the needs of the company with the time, resources, and staff needed to reach company objectives. Even the best managers run into obstacles along the way because it's often hard to determine just how much of an impact a project will have with minimal data.

There are also many models and ideas out there to help with this specific issue, but many of them fail to take all the necessary input and data - or the big picture - into account. This is where my model excels.

Time is money

Companies have tried many ways to approach the prioritization process, whether it has to do with: choosing a new project, recruiting a new employee, or making a crucial business decision. Some of these approaches have been more successful than others but generally, they are time-consuming and a waste of money if they don't work out in the company's favor. I'll use a common example to explain my reasoning here: offsite brainstorming sessions.

Many of us have participated in those half-day, full-day, or multi-day brainstorming sessions. They usually involve flip charts and sometimes colored dots for voting on projects. I've found those sessions intimidating and exhausting. Perhaps you've been to those offsite locations where you go to a remote place, like a fort or a campground. You're spending so much energy just getting yourself there! You've told your loved ones you're going away to an exotic place for a couple of days. Now there's hype around this offsite. You've picked your best clothes even though you don't know what the afternoon activity is going to be. All of this stuff goes on, which is not wrong from a team-building perspective. Don't get me wrong, the team building aspect of the offsite endeavor is incredibly valuable.

However, when there is the perception of hype and investment in an offsite-type session, people start to psych themselves out and not say much. Overall, this is very costly and an incredible waste of time. What's worse, it has become somewhat of a rite-of-passage in corporate America, so that most managers feel an obligation to do things this way. I'm not sure why this type of approach became so popular, especially because the end-results are usually less than satisfactory. However, people seem determined to do this year after year.

Odds are, you feel this obligation to spend six or eight hours doing all these brainstorming activities because it is the business justification for the trip. Often, people start to get exhausted by the second hour and don't really retain much. While they're sitting there, they're not really present. They're not really engaging. They're just ticking the box off this periodic offsite. Furthermore, anything that is discussed is not memorialized. It's captured on flip charts with stickers or Post-it notes. Therefore, if people are not fully engaging in it and it's also isolated to this single day or offsite - then one week later they probably can't recollect what was discussed at the session – it was an ineffectual waste of resources all the way around. Again, please don't mistake my intentions, the team-building aspect of the offsite is incredibly valuable, but let's not confuse that with a prioritization session.

I'm not saying that sticking to the same approach isn't right, because finding a solution that works for you is all that matters. People are unique, and each company's needs are different. This becomes a problem when you're struggling to find a process that works for you - and simply sticking to the unofficial industry "standard" because that's what everyone does, isn't necessarily the right approach. Brainstorming can become a hugely problematic area for the company, because when decisions don't work out, it costs the company time. And as we all know - time is money.

If you already have things sorted in this area, then good for you but most people need a bit of help when it comes to making decisions. This can be because they don't have all the necessary data to make an informed decision. Or, at least, they think they don't. But what my model will prove is that you can approach almost any decision from a data-driven standpoint if you use the resources you have – namely, <u>the people around you</u>. My approach focuses almost exclusively on quantifiable data input. Not only does this save on time, which saves money, but it also greatly increases the chance of a positive outcome for the company.

Another factor that makes my model so attractive is that it negates the need for those offsite brainstorming sessions. You can theoretically capture everyone's thoughts now in terms of what they think about the value of each project. Then, you can do the exercise again in three months, so you can see the trajectory of how a project has increased or decreased in value. You know exactly what the person thought the first time you asked because you have the data. You have a repository of data that has longevity and goes well beyond a flipchart, because it has been digitized.

The HiPPO's Influence

In every company, in every department, there's a person who can be identified as the HiPPO. No, that isn't a jab at anyone's physical appearance, but a term describing the most influential or highest paid member of a group. The HiPPO (Highest Paid Person's Opinion) usually ranks higher than other staff's opinions, regardless of whether their idea or opinion is more valuable.

Typically, when it comes time to start making decisions, most people would naturally defer to the HiPPO and just go along with whatever they say. For example, let's look at a brainstorming session for an advertising agency who's trying to decide on a new marketing campaign for one of their clients. Let's say, for argument's sake, that the people in this brainstorming session are all pretty creative people. They come up with some possible ideas on how to approach the campaign. Now, a lot of these ideas might be good, some might even be great. But who makes the decision on which project they should ultimately choose? Who decides of these ideas, everyone provided, which one was the best? Ultimately, it's going to be the HiPPO (the creative director, for instance) that makes the final decision. And ordinarily, this system works for the company. The campaign will likely be successful enough, and meet most, or all, of the goals the company set out to reach for their client. Because the HiPPO would arguably be the person with the most experience in this given area - the person most capable of making the hard decisions. After all, that's what they're getting paid to do.

But - and this is a big "but" - the choice (or choices) made by the HiPPO weren't necessarily the best solution for their clients' goals. By "best," I mean a project that wouldn't just have met the needs of their ultimate goal, but a project that would have met or even exceeded those needs as well as met additional needs in the most efficient way possible. When a company is always going with what the HiPPO dictates, it also ensures that no other project even gets tested for possible success – thereby, furthering the belief that the HiPPO's ideas are always the right ones. In the absence of any other ideas being tried, it's easy to consider that their ideas are always right. Furthermore, if their idea is wrong, it is generally easy to blame something else in the equation as to the reason for the failure of the idea.

So how would one go about addressing this dynamic? You need to take the opinions of the whole group into account.

Steve Jobs said:

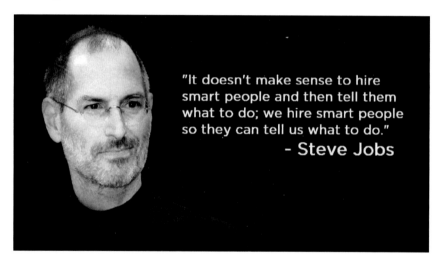

"It doesn't make sense to hire smart people and then tell them what to do; we hire smart people so they can tell us what to do."
- Steve Jobs

Never has this been truer than when it comes to making decisions, because the wisdom of the team as a collective is more valuable than the input of one individual. A project's value can be viewed from multiple angles, not just one person's personal perspective. Whenever I'm making decisions that will span across various departments, I always make sure to consult people in those departments. The reasoning behind this is quite simple; they know more about their department than I probably ever will. They know who can do what and when. They know which system works best for them to achieve their department's goals. They have a unique view on what their respective field can offer the company or where the company is lacking in that field. This is all invaluable information that I would never have, had I not taken the time to consult them.

Let data drive decisions, not the Highest Paid Person's Opinion.

At Tesla, where I was the Director of Digital Product, Design, and Content, I saw that the company functioned very similarly to the way Steve Jobs had run things. The highest paid person's opinion was what mattered, and we did what that person told us to do. That's not inherently a bad thing, because we had a visionary leader like Elon Musk to guide the way. Like Steve Jobs, Musk was often quite correct in what he wanted to see happen. Also, like Jobs, Musk valued having those smart people around him to help guide what to do and how to do it. He pushed people to do better work - to be great. Tesla currently operates from the perspective that Elon Musk is a genius, and his vision is incredible. It's a bit mind-blowing to look back on the number of times that I thought he was wrong about something, when, if you fast-forward months after that decision, it turns out that he was right. It's a humbling experience to go through because you're a skilled professional, and you think you know everything, or at least a lot. Then you find out that you were wrong almost 75% of the time.

You evolve so much over your career - you get educated, you work at wonderful places and grow your skills and knowledge. You find yourself in a position where you use conventional wisdom, you want to use your natural thought processes to make a decision, and you think you're smart. Then, someone like Elon Musk comes along. Even though I felt that some of those things he was pursuing or asking us to do might have been incorrect, it turns out that he was more right than wrong. So, at Tesla, the Team Decision Matrix model was rarely used because we already had someone driving the decision-making process. However, as I wrote before, the cases where that's a good thing are rare. This is why the Team Decision Matrix model is an important tool for most other cases that don't involve strong and visionary leaders like Jobs and Musk running the show.

I talked earlier about time being money, and many people would see this exercise as a waste of time and money. However, it has helped me get a well-rounded view on some very crucial decisions in the past. In the absence of a resource like the Team Decision Matrix, I am certain we would have made more arbitrary decisions which weren't rooted in data. I would have had to resort to gut feelings, which would have likely ended up with a low success rate.

Companies often spend too little time deciding what is right to build because they defer to the HiPPO. In the end, this can cost them dearly because when the HiPPO decides everything, there is little chance that you are always right. More than half the time people spend learning to inform the right ideas realized through the course of executing the wrong ideas. Unfortunately, companies don't have time for mistakes - especially when they're fueled by one person. So, it's a better solution for more people to give their collective input, since they would have collectively made more mistakes in the past, and learned from them. Thus, the wealth of knowledge offered is more than one individual could suggest.

The HiPPO's Far-Reaching Influence on Motivation

The other, darker part of the HiPPO's influence, is that you lose the ability to motivate people. Execution is so much harder than ideation, and by taking away the ability for the executors to ideate, you will lose your executors. People don't work as hard as when they're inspired and have their passions driving their efforts. If you just simply tell someone to do something, they might very well detach from it mentally or emotionally. They'll simply get it over with. I've seen this happen many times where things are strongly dictated to people. "Go do this and go do it by Thursday." The result of that type of directive is a very low emotional attachment to the quality of the projects being undertaken because that person didn't have a hand in the project's reason for existing. That person might not even believe that what they're doing is valuable. That puts them in a position where they just want to get the work over with - resulting in generally poor-quality work, low motivation to getting things done on time, and a low allegiance to the project outcome, among other factors.

By denying employees the opportunity to genuinely present ideas that they are passionate about, you're effectively losing out, on both, potentially good ideas and your team's ability to take responsibility for their work. Also, when people feel like they don't have the leeway to voice their opinions, then they become complacent with merely doing what you say and won't take any innovative steps with their work. Basically, there is a tremendous amount of trapped value in employees who are not incentivized, motivated, or expected to contribute to the company's success beyond executing what they are being told to do.

These people haven't been hired to be mindless robots that simply follow instructions, but when the HiPPO takes over, most people just become complacent and retreat into a role of subservience. In the end, the company loses out on the valuable resource that is human potential.

By utilizing the Team Decision Matrix method, employees from all departments are asked to take part and contribute toward products and projects that are or will be important to the company. When they are given this opportunity to express their opinions, influence a decision, or help decide what their next project will be, they feel productive and respected. This adds value to them as an employee; they will put this value back into the company through their work effort. It's a building exercise that works to add layers of confidence and respect from the bottom up.

The alignment of vision and process

The vision statement of a company usually comes from the CEO, or senior department leaders, who have a vision in mind for the company and strive to get that vision realized by the projects that each department tackles. How projects are approached is usually up to those that deal with the projects themselves, i.e., the company's employees. Prioritization happens at the team level - they're the ones who decide what they're going to do with the resources they have available to achieve the goals they've been given.

So how do you align this vision that upper management has set with the process so there's harmony between them? Frequently, companies build things that don't exactly match their intended goals, or they don't match the vision as much as they potentially could.

Companies may go for the SMART goal system when they're trying to make alignment of vision and process happen. You might already be familiar with this system (SMART stands for: Specific, Measurable, Achievable, Realistic, and Timely). It's a good system that generally makes sense.

Then there's also the OKR model (Objectives and Key Results), which major companies like Google and Twitter swear by. It provides a good framework for defining and tracking objectives, as well as their outcomes in a system that breaks down and cascades from one level to the next.

Then, you have the HiPPO. Now, I'm hammering so much on this topic because the HiPPO has such a significant influence on the prioritization process. The HiPPO is connected to the vision, and they may try their best to get the rest of the company to align with the vision. However, the HiPPO isn't always in tune with all the detailed minutiae of the inner workings of each department. It's not always feasible to know all the possible problems, opportunities, strategies, and tools available to you. I'm not saying this approach hasn't worked in the past. There are a lot of people out there who believe that the CEO or the senior leader is the one person who knows what's best for the company and that everyone should just do what that person says. And you do have your visionaries, like Steve Jobs and Elon Musk, who can drive a whole company to where they need it to be. I had the privilege of being able to interact with Elon from time-to-time, and it was truly a magical experience. Interacting with a person like him was very different from interacting with anyone else, because he is so insightful, and he knows the company down to its bones. People like Elon; they know where they are, where things need to go, and what needs to happen to get there. But these people are few and far between.

More than likely, you're going to get a HiPPO who wants to be insightful and thinks they know which course of action is best for the company, but who doesn't feel confident in their ability to drive the process alone - and that's because they can't. Not everyone can be a Steve Jobs. Let's look at Ron Johnson as an example. Ron Johnson worked with Target and Apple before taking on the role of CEO for JCPenney, and due to his successes at the other two large companies, the stock market foresaw success during his time with JCPenney. The valuation for JCPenney went up by about a billion dollars when he was announced as the CEO. He came in with established philosophies from Apple and Target which he tried to implement at a company that had already been working in a completely different way. He basically did away with the old pricing strategy and fired many of the company's top executives - which also meant they took all the institutional experience they had acquired with them.

The new pricing strategy that Ron introduced went directly against the data that JCPenney customers provided regarding what they wanted, which was discounted pricing. The mistake that Ron made was in thinking that he and his team had all the answers and that the current employees were incompetent. He fired some executives and rolled out a whole new plan that would "transform" the company. In the end, after working with JCPenney for 17 months, Ron left the company when sales went down by 25%, resulting in a net loss of $985 million and layoffs of over 17,000 people.

It's a tragic tale, but serves as a crucial warning about how much damage one person's decisions can do if they're given too much power over the direction of a company. More importantly, it shows what can happen if that person completely ignores the resident knowledge of the people of the company. It teaches us that using the HiPPO model isn't always the right thing to do. This is also a confusing story because Steve Jobs did all these things to turn Apple around and it worked. So why wouldn't it always work? Well, there are only a few Steve Jobs in a lifetime.

As a product manager, it can sometimes be hard to get around the HiPPO's effect. You want to include the HiPPO in the process because they provide the vision, the passion, and the ideologies that drive the process. But you also can't afford to have them take over completely. The Team Decision Matrix model has an effective way of dealing with the HiPPO, so they still give valuable input and make the big decisions, but the employees get to have their say as well. I will describe this when we get into the details of the model.

Roadmaps that lead to nowhere

As I wrote earlier, managers aren't dedicating enough time to prioritization. They simply see prioritization as a small step in the bigger roadmap. The problem is when the focus is on the roadmap, then it isn't on the individual parts that make up that roadmap. Many product managers also like to focus on the aesthetic beauty of their roadmaps rather than the substance. They rush through the prioritization part to get to the final roadmap. This is why roadmaps fail, because when you don't prioritize each feature based on value and cost, then the roadmap is meaningless.

Here's a common activity that all product managers have done at least once in their lives; they head to their computer, open Google, and search for a "roadmap template." They look at all the images and say, "I like this one best because it visually shows something that I can use when I'm standing in front of a room, so people think I know what I'm doing," or, "This is a good summary of a roadmap because it fits on one page." What they're really doing is looking at the aesthetic beauty of the roadmap. There's no valuable substance to it. It's all just based on different visual interpretations that present a collection of projects, timelines, and general themes, but they lack any quantitative depth. Here are some examples of some Google search results of "roadmap templates."

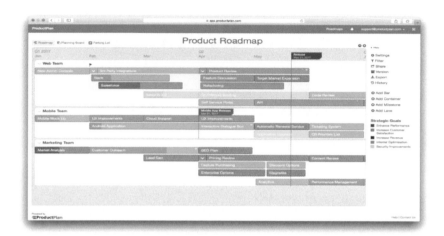

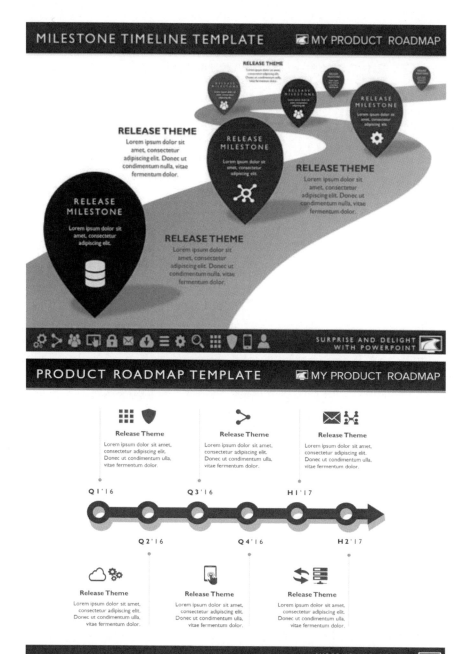

Roadmaps are undoubtedly important. They are, after all, a list of priorities, and as we've established, it's essential to prioritize. Roadmaps serve the purpose of connecting these various smaller tasks towards a larger goal. It stands to reason that the focus should be on making decisions around those smaller tasks rather than the overall roadmap. In contrast to what I stated earlier about small things getting in the way, we can also get hampered by the bigger picture. We tend to want to see the entire picture before we've filled in all the necessary details. We become overwhelmed by this huge project that we've taken on with seemingly no true direction to go in. Why is that? Usually, managers haven't taken the time to analyze all the data that they have available to justify both the project and each of the smaller tasks in that project. The roadmap feels empty despite being full of information.

Therefore, roadmaps should serve the function they are intended to serve - being a detailed compilation of priorities. However, the focus should always be on the prioritized tasks they contain and how these priorities relate to the ultimate goal. Relative to that, the Team Decision Matrix model has an in-depth analysis and rigor on value that's truly saying: these are the projects, this is the value, this is the investment it's going to take, these are the vectors it's going to move, this is who believes what amongst the people who decided on this roadmap. There are so many different things that this model shows you, that you forget about the visual element of the presentation. It focuses on what really matters, making people forget about this pretty slide that looks like a pipeline or street and that somehow gives the person who made it more credibility.

Key takeaways from this chapter:

In this chapter, I explained the main problems that arise when people try or fail to prioritize. One of the main issues of prioritization is the HiPPO's effect. The HiPPO is the highest paid person's opinion, and that person is usually the one calling the shots, whether they're backed by valuable data or not. Sometimes this works out well, like in the case of Steve Jobs. Other times it can have disastrous effects, like in the case of Ron Johnson. I've seen that the HiPPO's opinion is deferred to more often than not when it comes to making any decisions in the company, regardless of whether the employees may be able to offer valuable opinions. This is that the group as a whole can more effectively prioritize valuable tasks and projects through their collective experiences and knowledge than one person can. It's always better to utilize your assets - and people are assets. They were hired to be assets to the company after all, instead of people who just do what they're told.

In the next chapter, I will explain how the Team Decision Matrix model works in detail and provide some real-life examples from times when my model helped turn a crucial decision-making process into a much less stressful and time-consuming experience.

Chapter 2

RANK AND PRIORITIZE ANYTHING WITH THIS MODEL

As far as I can tell, there's currently no other model that encompasses both, the in-depth scope and simplicity of the Team Decision Matrix model. As I wrote in the introduction of this book, data is necessary for making informed decisions. However, what do you do when you don't have loads of data available to you, and you're running out of time? Unfortunately, this is the plight of many managers, and it isn't due to mismanagement or lack of experience.

Any manager can run into a snag, especially if you are truly innovating and are traversing in unchartered waters, where you may not have any definitive data at your fingertips. This usually results in a lack of confidence in the chosen project and some disconnect regarding which tasks are more crucial than others. Sometimes, if a project or idea isn't supported enough by upper management, that lack of confidence filters through to other employees, resulting in lethargy and lack of passion for the work. And why wouldn't it? No one wants to work on a project that they don't believe in or that they feel will fail.

The issue here is that, whenever managers have to face a crucial decision, they often think that they don't have enough information at hand to help them make the necessary choices. Also, they tend to think that they have to take the whole thing on by themselves. This is a huge undertaking, especially in large companies where one person is overseeing multiple teams of people. This results in unnecessary stress because the company didn't just hire one person - they hired many, and that collective has the power to provide the support a manager needs to make informed decisions in a relatively short amount of time. I have faced similar issues in the past where I have had to oversee a lot of people and keep track of the projects they're working on. During my time as head of product at StubHub, I oversaw 17 teams that were made up of about eight people each. I was only one person with a finite number of hours in the day, so how did I keep track of 17 teams and their roadmaps? The Team Decision Matrix gave me the data to do so. I could see exactly how everyone on each team was thinking, and I had all the data on the project list to know why they chose what they chose.

My model addresses the above concerns, through a democratized crowdsource-esque approach, that helps managers collect the necessary information to produce a data-driven roadmap, especially when there is no data. One of the biggest benefits to this model, especially when working with big groups of people, is that it allows you to re-use the data you've gathered over and over. This is an important concept in and of itself. Because it ties to the problems that you usually associate with brainstorming meetings, especially those "offsite collaboration" meetings we all loathe. By sustaining the use of this model, you can see how you have rated projects over time. You can memorialize the assessment of projects through the data captured, rather than during the offsite - which usually consists of post-it notes, flip charts, etc., and traps the value at that time in the hope that someone recorded it or remembers it.

That same data can still be used, even if the company's main goal for that quarter or year has changed. This effectively makes it a very flexible way of managing ideas and projects without taking up more of people's time.

Truthfully, the only hard part of this model is identifying the most valuable contributors to this prioritization process, which may or may not differ every time you start the process.

Step 1: Choosing Contributors

The first and most important step in this model starts with identifying a group of contributors to the prioritization process. In software development, this is typically the Product Manager, User Experience Designer, Engineering Manager, Quality Assurance, Project Manager, and other engineers involved in the project. I can also use an example outside of the software development context here since this model isn't meant to be used in that one context alone. In a marketing context, for example, the contributors might consist of the head of PR, the Social Media Manager, Content Writer, Brand Manager, Paid Search Specialist, Market Researcher, etc. Of course, you'll be much better equipped to identify the best contributors for your needs and so I won't presume to know better and try to dictate your choices here.

However, I will say that it's a good idea to gather a group of diverse job disciplines that can view the options you present from multiple angles so the feedback you get is all-encompassing rather than narrowed down.

Of course, there is also such a thing as selecting a too-diverse group. The people you choose need to be at least somewhat familiar with the parameters you provided and be able to give knowledgeable feedback on the subject. For instance, you wouldn't necessarily choose an accountant as a contributor to prioritize new web functions for the company website, unless you think that person might have some unique insight to offer.

You might be wondering how many contributors to choose. Generally, I would say there's no wrong number to go with here. However, the minimum number of contributors needed for this model to get an effective input is five. Five serves as a reliable minimum depending on how many factors you need to take into account and across how many departments the decision will have an effect. If, however, you're using the model to prioritize "smaller" decisions in a more personal sphere, like where to go on vacation, then you don't need many contributors. You only need yourself and perhaps one other contributor; if you plan to consult a spouse, for example. I'll get more into that a bit later when I discuss how the model can be used for any purposes outside of product management. For now, let's stick with five as the minimum number of contributors needed to make this model function properly. Sometimes you'll need many more contributors to get accurate feedback about which priorities rank higher than others. The point is, it's all up to how you want to adapt it to fit your needs.

Using the Team Decision Matrix model, I'll add five example contributors that I've named Sudhir, Jaclyn, Marcus, Karlyn, and Corey. These five people will help choose the next feature to add to their company's e-commerce store.

Here's what that would look like on a spreadsheet:

Contributors
Sudhir
Jaclyn
Marcus
Karlyn
Corey

Step 2: Identify the Vectors of Value

After choosing the contributors that will suit the purposes of your prioritization process, you'll need to define the most important vectors of value for this given project or decision. You'll be assigning a percentage value (out of 100%) to each vector you choose, and the weight of each will be determined by how critical one vector is when compared to the other vectors. These vectors will ultimately determine which project, or decision, you go with. They are the indicators from which the contributors will base their decisions.

I spoke a bit earlier about managing the HiPPO's decisions and expectations when it comes to this process. Well here's how I do it: I let them decide the value of each vector. A CEO or senior manager wants to feel in control of what their employees are doing and when they're not part of the decision-making process, they usually feel out of control. What I do is present them with the vectors I've chosen (which should align with the company goals or any goals they specifically want to reach with this product/project) and give them the space to decide which vectors "weigh" more heavily than others. In addition to giving them the option to assign each vector a value, you can always just let the HiPPO decide on which vectors are applicable from the start. That way, you give them even more control over how the process aligns with their vision without letting them dictate the entire course of the process. It is important to channel the HiPPO towards vectors which are actionable and measurable at a team level. I have found that using Revenue, Sales or Market Share are too high level of which any one specific project may not be able to influence.

After defining the vectors and giving each a value percentage, you will present them to the contributors so they can rank them from most important to least important. I'll discuss how exactly that happens in step 3. But the most important thing you need to remember here is that your contributors don't need to know the respective weights you've assigned to each vector. They simply must choose which vectors they deem more important than others, and you can then base your calculations off of that without influencing their decisions.

The vectors you choose will differ from business to business and also from one situation to another. For example, the vectors chosen by a Product Manager, in a major tech company, won't be the same vectors chosen by a Marketing

Manager for that same company.

Below is an example of 5 vectors that I've chosen for the e-commerce experience:

Business Score Weighting	
Increase Conversion	35%
Increase Traffic	25%
Net Promoter Score	5%
Lead Generation	25%
Increase average order size	10%
	100%

Some vectors the Marketing Manager might consider include: brand awareness, purchase intent, lead capture, product knowledge, and repeat purchase.

Here's what that would look like:

Business Score Weighting	
Brand Awareness	35%
Purchase Intent	25%
Lead Capture	5%
Product Knowledge	25%
Repeat Purchase	10%
	100%

Instead of trying to explain what vectors are, and how to choose them, I will give you an example of how they work. Hopefully, this will help you get the right idea about what these vectors mean and what sort of vectors you should be looking at to suit your own company's needs.

I believe that you must pick vectors which are the drivers of revenue, profit, and market share. If one achieves growth in revenue, profit or market share, then arguably shareholder value increases. Let's say that for this example, I've decided that the company wants to focus on gaining new revenue through its online platform. So, my business score weighting above will reflect which vectors I think will help me achieve that goal.

This vector system is one of the features that make me proud to show off this model. The amazing thing about assigning percentages to these vectors is that they aren't set in stone. These vectors can easily be adjusted to accommodate changes to a business. For example, if the business focus changes one week, one month, or one quarter later, it allows you to simply change the percentages without having to change the scoring. This is a critical point that I will expand upon later.

After you've identified the most important vectors you want to work with and given each of them the respective business score weights that correspond with your goals, you can move on to identifying the features (or projects) that you want to present to your contributors.

Step 3: Identify the Features

Before you can start getting feedback from your contributors, you first must have something to show them. After all, people can't judge the impact a project will potentially have on the vectors you've outlined if you don't have any projects to show them. The features you choose to use in the Team Decision Matrix model will depend on which method you prefer for choosing projects. Every company and every manager has their own way of gathering and organizing employee suggestions and project ideas.

After you've identified the features you want to use for this round, you can start listing them in preparation for the session with your contributors. I prefer using a spreadsheet myself, but you can use any program or method you're comfortable with, including the Reviewscale product within Ideascale. The only real rule here is to make sure that you describe the essence of each feature within 140 characters (a small nod to those original Twitter users). The 140-character limit helps keep the product managers, or whoever is describing the projects, as clear and concise as possible. This part should be written in layman's terms so that anyone in the company can generally understand the feature. In the example below, the project name is "Rewards – status and enrollment" which is basically allowing the user of an e-commerce site (in this case it was StubHub) to see what level of rewards they have reached and what will happen when they reach the next level. The description offered in the cell note is brief, clear and specific.

12	User Account preferences	0.9
13	Rewards - status and enrollment	1.7
14	Surface primary listings (e.g. AEG, MLB, Pac)	0.5
15	SH Digital Ticket - next phase - partnerships	1.6
16	Sell flow Improvements - Re-list ticket via apps	2.8

Product Manager: rewards details – what customers have, how can they reach next level etc

Step 4: Start the Session

All the prep work is done. Now it's time to gather your contributors together and put them to work judging each feature. Each contributor should indicate the impact they think each of the features will have across all the vectors you've chosen.

Here's how the process should ideally go:

- Get everyone in a room together, don't let them talk about project ideas or have them see any of the project features you're going to present beforehand.

This is important because you really just want to aim for everyone's top-of-mind reactions at this point. Whereas any info revealed previously could be used to game the system before the scoring begins. (And yes, you certainly will encounter people who try to game the system. I have a good example of a time when this happened to me which I'll describe later on in this book when I talk about exercising caution.)

- Present the first idea or project to your contributors. You should try to stick to the 140-word description, so afford around 30 seconds for each feature description. None of the contributors should give their input on any of the features out loud or discuss a feature after you've described it. The reason for this is simple: you don't want any members of the group being influenced by any sort of bias that may surface during a discussion. Any discussions can happen after the scoring phase is finished.

- Each contributor should then receive a copy of the spreadsheet (preferably digitally to make things easier for you later). They should then silently assess their perceived business value for each vector you've listed next to the project you've just presented. Each vector should be given a Small, Medium, Large, or No Impact assessment. This shouldn't take more than 30 seconds - you don't want people thinking it through too much, just their top-of-mind reaction.

- After everyone has given their assessment, you move on to the description of the next feature, and then the contributors assess that project according to the vectors as well. This process should be repeated for each feature you've listed.

After a full session of scoring is complete, you'll likely see a summary for one contributor which resembles this:

Sudhir		35%	25%		5%	25%	10%
# Project	Conversion	NPS		Cost Savings	Traffic	Inventory
1 Go Together (Web view)	M	M		-	L	-
2 Recommendations data input from fan	-	-		-	-	-
3 Recommendations data output to fan	L	L		-	S	-
4 Optimize Android tablet layouts	S	M		-	S	-
5 LMS Ticket finder	S	S		S	S	-
6 Gift card redemption	-	S		S	S	-
7 One-time dismissable ""new user"" app overlay	S	M		S	-	S
8 Expanded band and venue data should be available. (Enhanced content	-	M		-	S	-
9 Shopping cart	M	M		S	-	-
10 Group chat / sharing pre/at/post event	-	L		-	M	-
11 Consolidated Universal Mobile Tracking/Metrics	M	M		S	-	S
12 User Account preferences	M	M		-	-	-
13 Rewards - status and enrollment	M	M		S	M	-
14 Surface primary listings (e.g. AEG, MLB, Pac)	-	-		-	-	-
15 SH Digital Ticket - next phase - partnerships	S	L		-	S	-
16 Sell flow Improvements - Re-list ticket via apps	M	M		M	M	L
17 Enhanced map layers - heat maps for pricing analysis	M	M		-	M	S
18 My Account revamp - with new gateway APIs	S	M		M	M	S
19 Add to user's calendar	-	S		M	-	-
20 Enhanced map - Social friends	M	M		-	S	-
21 User generated content - pictures, videos, reviews	-	M		-	L	-
22 Fan check-in	-	S		-	S	-
23 Digital Scrapbook/Sharing	S	M		-	L	-

During each assessment, you also need to give the leading contributor from each department (so the Engineering Lead,

QA Lead, etc., for instance) a second objective. They need to indicate the level of effort or cost that they deem will be necessary for each project as well. It's best to do this when each project is being evaluated for its business value so these leaders can have the context in mind when they are offering their reaction to the level of effort it will cost from their respective groups. Again, they shouldn't take too much time to think this through. You just need their impressions that are at the forefront of their minds. Ultimately, there's going to be one or two departments who will serve as the main decision-makers when it comes to project effort for each project on your list.

When it comes to those working in software development, my experience has taught me that engineering effort is probably the best indicator of effort from UX and QA. But to be inclusive of all functional teams, it is best to include them so you can get a well-rounded resource planning view. More on the resource planning view later, though. When it comes to determining effort for a project, you'll need to ask your contributors to relate to each project in a quantifiable way. Engineering effort is typically viewed in the context of "development days", for instance. When it comes to calculating the value of small, medium and large, I used 1, 3, and 5 respectively for each effort size. This correlates to development days, which in my example, I've assumed to be 12, 24, and 48 days to denote the project size differences. So, in the example, I would then ask Marcus to assign values of either 1, 3, or 5 against each feature.

The values assigned to small, medium, and large effort sizes for each project.

Engineering Effort	Pts
S	1
M	3
L	5

When giving your department leaders this task, make sure to be specific about what value you're giving to the small, medium, and large variables. Also, make sure that they know how that will relate to the effort they've outlined for their department so they can respond accordingly. For example, in Engineering, that would translate to the number of days needed to complete the project.

However, the small, medium, and large effort sizes would translate to quantifiable data for a department like

Engineering Development.

Engineering dev	days
S	12
M	24
L	48

The whole session up until this point should have progressed with as much silence from the contributors as possible. There should be no discussion about any of the projects along the way. I say this because people influence each other's decisions. And with this model, your goal is to get everyone's top of mind assessment on each feature before they're clouded by discussion and everyone's opinions weaving together. This also completely cancels out the potential influence of any HiPPO in the room, should one be present.

After all of the contributors have submitted their assessments, then you're welcome to let everyone in the room discuss the projects and present their opinions. You've already gathered the valuable input you wanted, and any additional feedback could potentially be just as valuable a contribution - especially if there's a great flow of energy between the group and they start bouncing ideas off one another. Never try to stifle creativity or enthusiasm because some of the best ideas are born that way and you can make a note of any meaningful suggestions made during this period of the meeting. If, however, you're not interested in a lengthy discussion around the ideas that you've presented then you thank everyone for their time, end the meeting, and move on to the next phase.

Step 5: How to analyze the data that you've gathered

Once you have collected all the input from the contributors, you can do a couple of things. It's easier to use a spreadsheet format (like the provided examples) because that allows you to accurately keep track of all the information you've gathered. It's a good visual representation that will also allow you to easily calculate the values of each project and even change the outcome of the data by changing the vectors as needed. This also means that you won't have to go back and repeat the whole process if you ever decide to change any or all the vectors' score weightings. This makes it easy when working with a HiPPO who may want to change the vector scores later or frequently. Even if that person decides to change the vector weightings after the project scoring process has been completed, the data remains reliable. Because the contributors didn't know the weightings assigned to each vector when they were scoring the projects, so their opinions still hold true. The only things that change now are the average business scores assigned to each project.

Of course, the same cannot be said for changing the vectors themselves. All the data you've gathered is unique to these vectors, and once you've collected the input from your contributors, you won't be able to change any of the vectors without starting the process all over again. But changing vector weight won't change the integrity of contributor assessments since they never even knew the respective weight of each vector in the first place.

Before you get started, you need to make sure to give the weightings your contributors used during their assessment a business value. Here's an example:

Business value	Pts
S	1
M	3
L	9
-	0

Now, here's what you can do with the data you've gathered.

Determine Overall Business Value: The overall business value is the weighted average against each vector and the sum average of each contributor all rolled up into one number. This basically shows you a 1 to N ranking of each project against each other. This is purely the value of the project. Be careful that you are not taking this literally. For example, you shouldn't consider project number 21 to be absolutely better than project number 22 on the list. Rather, the top half of the projects or top 20% are generally higher value than the bottom half or bottom 20%.

Here's what the unsorted average business score would look like:

ID#	Project	Business Score Avg Biz Score	Biz Score Std De
1	Go Together (Web view)	3.6	2.0
2	Recommendations data input from fan	0.3	0.4
3	Recommendations data output to fan	4.6	1.7
4	Optimize Android tablet layouts	1.1	0.7
5	LMS Ticket finder	0.7	0.4
6	Gift card redemption	0.8	0.4
7	One-time dismissable ""new user"" app overlay.	0.8	0.4
8	Expanded band and venue data should be available. (Enhanced	2.0	0.7
9	Shopping cart	2.5	1.4
10	Group chat / sharing pre/at/post event	1.8	1.0
11	Consolidated Universal Mobile Tracking/Metrics	1.2	0.8
12	User Account preferences	0.8	0.7
13	Rewards - status and enrollment	1.7	0.6
14	Surface primary listings (e.g. AEG, MLB, Pac)	0.5	0.8
15	SH Digital Ticket - next phase - partnerships	1.6	1.1
16	Sell flow Improvements - Re-list ticket via apps	2.8	1.6
17	Enhanced map layers - heat maps for pricing analysis	1.4	0.9
18	My Account revamp - with new gateway APIs	1.0	0.7
19	Add to user's calendar	0.9	0.7
20	Enhanced map - Social friends	1.6	1.6
21	User generated content - pictures, videos, reviews	2.3	0.5
22	Fan check-in	0.7	0.6
23	Digital Scrapbook/Sharing	1.6	1.0

Calculate Contributors Comparison/Standard Deviation:
This is the level of variance that the contributors have between their assessment of each project. If all contributors are within a close range of their assessment, then the standard deviation will be low. This suggests the level of cohesion that the group of contributors feels on projects. So, if you find a high-value project, but a high standard deviation, it is worth unpacking why there is such a variance amongst your people.

In my experience, this is most often explained by the level of familiarity people have with each project, or there might have been a misunderstanding. Sometimes, a contributor has better data or insight than the rest of the group, and since there hadn't been an opportunity to discuss the projects during the assessment phase, it's reasonable to see wide variances in some cases. So, if I'm the decision-maker here, I would look at the most highly rated projects on the spreadsheet, the top 3, and look at their standard deviation. Because I have data now which exposes the level of disagreement on those projects and, if there's a high level of disagreement from anyone on the team, now would be the time to discuss it.

I usually take the projects that have a high standard deviation and arrange another meeting with the group to discuss why they gave each project the values that they did.

Here's what it would typically look like if you have some projects with higher standard deviations, where you can clearly see who is above or below the rest of the group for each project. You can be assured that this view of data will result in some robust dialogue.

ID#	Project	Avg Biz Score	Biz Score Std De	Contributors - Business Score				
				Sudhir	Jaclan	Marcus	Karlan	Corea
1	Go Together (Web view)	3.6	2.0	4.1	1.0	6.3	2.6	4.1
3	Recommendations data output to fan	4.6	1.7	5.7	6.3	4.8	1.9	4.7
9	Shopping cart	2.5	1.4	1.9	1.0	3.4	4.5	1.9
16	Sell flow Improvements - Re-list ticket via apps	2.8	1.6	3.6	1.2	2.5	5.1	1.7
20	Enhanced map - Social friends	1.6	1.6	2.1	4.2	0.3	0.9	0.9
30	Native checkout (Guest checkout)	4.5	1.8	5.5	6.0	3.6	5.8	1.9
39	Create urgency for buyers	1.3	1.3	3.4	1.7	0.4	0.5	0.4
40	Seat upgrade	1.2	1.4	3.4	1.5	0.3	0.4	0.3
43	Promotions API integration with iTunes & Android	1.5	1.4	3.6	2.2	0.0	0.9	0.9
46	Location and distance	1.6	1.6	0.6	4.3	2.1	0.6	0.6
64	Native Checkout phase 3 - 1-click (PayPal API integration)	1.8	1.6	4.4	1.0	0.0	2.0	1.9
69	Links - open directly on apps	1.5	1.6	1.9	0.0	4.1	0.6	0.8
76	Live event page - scores / comments /	1.2	1.3	0.5	1.0	3.4	0.8	0.3
80	Paypal incentives	2.1	1.6	2.7	1.0	4.6	1.0	1.4
82	Branded FanZone + Cisco's StadiumVision	3.1	1.4	4.5	2.0	4.9	1.9	2.5
83	App A/B testing frameword	3.4	1.7	3.8	3.8	5.9	1.4	2.1
86	Gifting of ticket	1.8	1.6	1.4	4.4	0.3	1.9	1.2
89	Post - provide integrated storage for photos / videos -	1.2	2.6	0.0	5.8	0.0	0.0	0.0
91	Price Alerts without idenity	2.7	2.2	2.1	2.9	6.2	0.5	1.6

I use the contributor comparison to be the basis for the discussion because you can ensure that you are talking about the projects where there is a disagreement in the assessed value. What often happens when people aren't agreeing on a project in "planning sessions?" You've probably been in a couple of these yourself, where you get a bunch of post-it notes, and you put them on a whiteboard. Everyone gets a bunch of stickers to vote with and hours go by where everyone's exhausted and wants to be done with it by the second hour. The Team Decision Matrix approach is nothing like that. You now have the data to make a calculated discussion happen. You can get to the bottom line of what the data tells you and discuss where you're aligned on value and misaligned on opinions. This means that the root of the difference in opinion can be found quickly and the matter resolved.

To some extent, you also need to discuss the projects that everyone agrees are of low value - as there is consensus and the score is low. This point alone is so powerful because many teams spend time discussing projects which hold no value to anyone in the group. You can gain some insight here on why the team deems these projects of low value, which can be useful and save a lot of time in future discussions. Of the projects which have the lowest value, there is a consensus amongst the contributors on their low value, like in the example below:

Calculate the ROI score: Equally as important as the value of the project are the resources needed to complete a project. It's not just about what you get out of it, after all, but also what you must put in to achieve the result. The model can help in this regard too, because it can help determine how you should best allocate your resources.

ID#	Project	Avg Biz Score	Biz Score Std De	Sudhir	Jaclan	Marcus	Karlan	Cores
2	Recommendations data input from fan	0.3	0.4	0.0	1.0	0.0	0.5	0.1
5	LMS Ticket finder	0.7	0.4	0.9	1.2	0.4	0.3	0.5
6	Gift card redemption	0.8	0.4	0.6	1.5	0.7	0.6	0.9
7	One-time dismissable ""new user"" app overlay.	0.8	0.4	1.3	1.0	0.3	0.7	0.6
12	User Account preferences	0.8	0.7	1.8	1.0	0.3	0.5	0.3
14	Surface primary listings (e.g. AEG, MLB, Pac)	0.5	0.8	0.0	1.8	0.0	0.5	0.0
18	My Account revamp - with new gateway APIs	1.0	0.7	2.1	1.0	0.3	1.2	0.7
19	Add to user's calendar	0.9	0.7	0.4	1.0	2.1	0.6	0.5
22	Fan check-in	0.7	0.6	0.5	1.5	0.3	1.1	0.3
24	Google / Paypal / Samsung Wallet support	1.0	0.5	1.4	1.5	0.3	1.0	1.0
25	In venue beacon support	1.0	0.9	0.5	1.0	0.6	0.5	2.5
27	Home Screen Redesign	0.0	0.0	0.0	0.0	0.0	0.0	0.0
32	iOS7 re-design	0.0	0.0	0.0	0.0	0.0	0.0	0.0
33	Mobile entry - SH template optimized for mobile	0.0	0.0	0.0	0.0	0.0	0.0	0.0
34	Tracking improvements (Fiksu, Omniture, Flurry)	0.7	0.8	1.9	1.0	0.0	0.5	0.1
37	Show calendar view of events	1.0	0.7	1.1	2.2	0.6	0.6	0.4
38	Customer service features - chat / SMS on app	0.8	0.6	1.1	1.5	0.0	0.8	0.6
41	Scan calendar & email for purchases	0.9	0.5	1.6	1.0	1.2	0.5	0.4
44	Buy Pricing guidance - Sold tickets	0.9	0.7	0.6	2.2	0.4	1.0	0.5
45	Viral coupon sharing	0.0	0.0	0.0	0.0	0.0	0.0	0.0
51	Fraud integration with APIs	0.6	0.5	0.5	1.4	0.5	0.5	0.1
52	CS - Tealeaf - rich mobile interaction data with screenshots	0.5	0.3	0.5	1.0	0.4	0.4	0.1
53	Split with friends	0.3	0.7	0.0	1.5	0.0	0.0	0.0

As a decision-maker, you need to know the costs you're going to bear on each project so you can make the assessment of value relative to cost. When you go buy a car or go to the grocery store, you look at value relative to cost - everywhere you go, you rate the value against cost. For some reason, however, people tend not to do that when they make decisions in the business environment. This model enables you to do so. With the ROI score (short for "return on investment"), you know the value you're going to get relative to the investment or time to market.

The ROI calculation is the business value score divided by the engineering level of effort. So, sticking with our software development example, let's say that a business value score of 6.0, for instance, divided by an engineering size of Medium (3.0) would equate to an ROI score 2.0. This is an interesting calculation, because a project which has a lower business value, say 3.0, with an engineering size of small (1.0) would have an ROI value of 3.0. This calculation is not absolute, as you may not want to pursue only small engineering sized projects. If you did, you risk iterating on small things rather than making a big impact. But, if you have a timeline or target and need to know which projects can be executed in a short timeframe and you would need to balance the value across various sized projects, this is a good way to look at things. Below is an example of what a spreadsheet would look like with the calculated ROI score next to the business score. In particular, look at project ID #1 and #3. Project #3 has a definitively higher average business score than Project #1, but when you look at the ROI score, which is the average business score divided by the engineering cost, you get a vastly different picture. Project #1 seems to deliver in a faster timeframe than Project #3. Though, as I look at this data, I also notice that the Biz Score Standard Deviation is quite high, so it seems these projects are worth discussing before deciding between.

ID#	Project	Business Score		ROI - Biz Score	
		Avg Biz Score	Biz Score Std De	ROI Biz Score	ROI Std De
1	Go Together (Web view)	3.6	2.0	3.6	2.0
2	Recommendations data input from fan	0.3	0.4	0.1	0.1
3	Recommendations data output to fan	4.6	1.7	0.9	0.3
4	Optimize Android tablet layouts	1.1	0.7	0.4	0.2
5	LMS Ticket finder	0.7	0.4	0.2	0.1
6	Gift card redemption	0.8	0.4	0.2	0.1
7	One-time dismissable ""new user"" app overlay.	0.8	0.4	0.8	0.4
8	Expanded band and venue data should be available. (Enhanced	2.0	0.7	0.4	0.1
9	Shopping cart	2.5	1.4	0.5	0.3
10	Group chat / sharing pre/at/post event	1.8	1.0	0.4	0.2
11	Consolidated Universal Mobile Tracking/Metrics	1.2	0.8	0.4	0.3
12	User Account preferences	0.8	0.7	0.2	0.1
13	Rewards - status and enrollment	1.7	0.6	0.6	0.2
14	Surface primary listings (e.g. AEG, MLB, Pac)	0.5	0.8	0.2	0.3
15	SH Digital Ticket - next phase - partnerships	1.6	1.1	0.3	0.2
16	Sell flow Improvements - Re-list ticket via apps	2.8	1.6	0.6	0.3
17	Enhanced map layers - heat maps for pricing analysis	1.4	0.9	0.5	0.3
18	My Account revamp - with new gateway APIs	1.0	0.7	0.2	0.1
19	Add to user's calendar	0.9	0.7	0.9	0.7
20	Enhanced map - Social friends	1.6	1.6	0.5	0.5
21	User generated content - pictures, videos, reviews	2.3	0.5	0.5	0.1
22	Fan check-in	0.7	0.6	0.1	0.1

Because you already know the ROI score of each project, you can make an informed decision on which actions to take so your goals are reached within the relative timeframe. If you're trying to achieve deadlines or maybe you have holiday time coming up, and you want to get one more project done before everyone leaves, this view allows you to see the value relative to the engineering cost. Say you want to start on a project that's for Christmas, but it can only be completed by

February. Does that hold any value for you? No. Meaning you find another project with nearly equal value that you know your team will be able to complete in time to impact Christmas. The model makes this process straightforward and puts all the data you need right there in front of you for easy comparison.

Identify the vector sort order: Sometimes a company needs to focus their efforts on one thing to reach their goals. When I was at StubHub, focusing on conversion was of paramount importance. Luckily, this model is versatile and allows you to sort projects on the basis of their value against each vector. This is particularly good as you can see their impact on the vectors that matter most to you. Of course, you could always change the weighting to be 100% towards conversion (in the case at StubHub), which will essentially allow you to see which projects count the most towards that one vector, according to your contributors. But then you wouldn't see whether any of the other projects, with the exact same impact on conversion, may also have an effect on another vector.

While you may only care about conversion, choosing a project which also impacts traffic, for instance, will let you get a bonus benefit of more traffic, too. This way of organizing the project list allows you to see projects through a different lens, as well as choose projects that can potentially exceed CEO and shareholder expectations. The example below shows how you can focus on conversion, but also see which other vectors the projects will impact.

ID#	Project	Contributors Conversion Avg Conversion Score (Unweighte	Contributors NPS Avg NPS Score (Unweighte	Contributors Cost Savings Avg Cost Savings Score (Unweighte	Contributors Traffic Avg Traffic Score (Unweighte	Contributors Inventory mgmt Avg Inventory mgmt Score (Unweighte
1	Go Together (Web view)	3.8	3.8	0.2	5.0	0.4
2	Recommendations data input from fan	0.2	0.4	0.4	0.4	0.2
3	Recommendations data output to fan	7.4	5.4	0.2	2.6	0.4
4	Optimize Android tablet layouts	1.2	1.8	0.4	0.8	0.2
5	LMS Ticket finder	0.4	1.0	0.6	0.6	0.8
6	Gift card redemption	0.8	1.4	0.8	0.6	0.2
7	One-time dismissable ""new user"" app overlay.	0.8	1.4	0.6	0.2	0.4
8	Expanded band and venue data should be	2.0	3.0	0.4	1.8	0.4
9	Shopping cart	5.0	2.2	0.6	0.4	0.8
10	Group chat / sharing pre/at/post event	0.8	3.4	0.2	2.6	0.2
11	Consolidated Universal Mobile Tracking/Metrics	1.4	2.0	1.4	0.4	0.6
12	User Account preferences	0.8	1.4	0.2	0.4	0.2
13	Rewards - status and enrollment	2.2	1.8	0.6	1.4	0.8
14	Surface primary listings (e.g. AEG, MLB, Pac)	0.4	0.2	0.2	0.2	2.0
15	SH Digital Ticket - next phase - partnerships	1.2	3.0	1.0	1.2	1.2
16	Sell flow Improvements - Re-list ticket via apps	2.2	3.4	2.2	2.2	5.4
17	Enhanced map layers - heat maps for pricing	1.2	2.2	0.4	1.2	1.0
18	My Account revamp - with new gateway APIs	0.6	1.8	1.2	1.0	0.6
19	Add to user's calendar	1.0	1.2	0.8	0.8	0.2
20	Enhanced map - Social friends	1.6	3.0	0.2	1.2	0.2
21	User generated content - pictures, videos, reviews	1.2	3.0	0.2	4.2	0.2
22	Fan check-in	0.4	1.6	0.2	0.6	0.2

Calculate the revenue impact: In commerce businesses, if you can increase conversion and/or traffic, you increase revenue. To clarify, it's hard to increase both of these at the same time, but sometimes it does happen. The StubHub mobile app was one of these cases. Regarding the prioritization of projects at StubHub, the inputs from each of the contributors can be used to assess a general Small, Medium, or Large impact on traffic and conversion.

An example, here is what the spreadsheet would look like with the calculated revenue impact for each project next to its business score and ROI score. All this data together gives a well-rounded view to approach each project and will help make the process of choosing a project completely data-driven. That way, you can approach anyone and justify any decision that's been made.

ID#	Project	Business Score		ROI - Biz Score		Incremental Revenue Impact	
		Avg Biz Score	Biz Score Std De	ROI Biz Score	ROI Std De	Avg. Inc Rev Impact	Inc Rev St De
1	Go Together (Web view)	3.6	2.0	3.6	2.0	166	126
2	Recommendations data input from fan	0.3	0.4	0.1	0.1	11	20
3	Recommendations data output to fan	4.6	1.7	0.9	0.3	240	155
4	Optimize Android tablet layouts	1.1	0.7	0.4	0.2	57	54
5	LMS Ticket finder	0.7	0.4	0.2	0.1	20	25
6	Gift card redemption	0.8	0.4	0.2	0.1	38	24
7	One-time dismissable ""new user"" app overlay.	0.8	0.4	0.8	0.4	37	24
8	Expanded band and venue data should be available. (Enhanced	2.0	0.7	0.4	0.1	99	61
9	Shopping cart	2.5	1.4	0.5	0.3	172	108
10	Group chat / sharing pre/at/post event	1.8	1.0	0.4	0.2	50	60
11	Consolidated Universal Mobile Tracking/Metrics	1.2	0.8	0.4	0.3	64	66
12	User Account preferences	0.8	0.7	0.2	0.1	38	55
13	Rewards - status and enrollment	1.7	0.6	0.6	0.2	106	72
14	Surface primary listings (e.g. AEG, MLB, Pac)	0.5	0.8	0.2	0.3	19	20
15	SH Digital Ticket - next phase - partnerships	1.6	1.1	0.3	0.2	60	27
16	Sell flow Improvements - Re-list ticket via apps	2.8	1.6	0.6	0.3	111	75
17	Enhanced map layers - heat maps for pricing analysis	1.4	0.9	0.5	0.3	60	61
18	My Account revamp - with new gateway APIs	1.0	0.7	0.2	0.1	32	29
19	Add to user's calendar	0.9	0.7	0.9	0.7	48	56
20	Enhanced map - Social friends	1.6	1.6	0.5	0.5	78	75
21	User generated content - pictures, videos, reviews	2.3	0.5	0.5	0.1	74	60
22	Fan check-in	0.7	0.6	0.1	0.1	20	20
23	Digital Scrapbook/Sharing	1.6	1.0	0.3	0.2	30	34

If you have a handle on your commerce economics, then you have a mechanism to estimate the revenue impact of each project on the list. Suppose a medium lift in conversion is a 50-basis points increase, and a large lift in traffic is a 100-basis points increase. If the contributor group average suggests both a traffic and conversion lift, then you can predict the impact on revenue.

That might not entirely make sense to you yet, so let's go through the math on this:

Conversion lifts from 2.5% to 3.0% (50-basis points). If you have 2,000 orders typically at an average order size of $10, then you normally make $20,000 in gross revenue. With the 50-basis point increase, an incremental 100 orders (2,000 * .5). At $10 average order size, this would be $1,000 in new revenue associated with the project in question.

Similarly, if you typically get 100,000 visitors per day, and you get a 100-basis point (1%) lift in traffic from the project you are considering, then you can expect 1,000 incremental visitors. The 1,000 incremental visitors might have previously converted at 2.5%, but with this new feature they convert at 3%, so you would get an additional 30 orders on top of the 100 orders from the conversion only increase. So, this feature improved your orders by 130, which at $10 average order size, resulted in $1,300 in net new revenue from this project.

Here's an example of the baseline economics you'll need to make the type of calculation described above:

I'm going to put all of this together in an example for you so that you can see just how powerful this model can be if you gathered the data and started using it.

Baseline Inputs						
Mobile Visits	2,000,000 /mo					
Conversion %	1.8%					
Avg GTS	$204					
Avg. Profit Margin	22%					
Avg. Revenue	$45 /transaction					
Avg. Total GTS	$7,344,000 /mo					
Avg. Total Revenue	$1,615,680 /mo					

Size	Traffic Lift % Δ	Conversion Change		Traffic Lift #/mo	Conversion Rates
-	0.00%	0.00%		-	1.8%
S	0.25%	0.05%	3%	5,000	1.9%
M	1.00%	0.15%	8%	20,000	2.0%
L	2.00%	0.30%	17%	40,000	2.1%

$ Profit/mo Calculator

		Conversion Change			
		-	S	M	L
Traffic Lift	-	$ -	$ 44,880	$ 134,640	$ 269,280
	S	$ 4,039	$ 49,031	$ 139,016	$ 273,992
	M	$ 16,157	$ 61,486	$ 152,143	$ 288,130
	L	$ 32,314	$ 78,091	$ 169,646	$ 306,979

For instance, I have a list of decided-upon projects for the next quarter - a roadmap. What this allows me to do is see what the estimated revenue is per project. Let's say it's a million dollars per month from the time these projects are collectively released. So now I have a directional average revenue number for all these projects. In this example, I'm looking at a particular project that we want to take on next quarter with an estimated revenue value of $240,000. I also know exactly what everyone on the team thinks about each project. Let's say that in my example, Marcus doesn't think as highly of the project as the other people. I can now go to Marcus and ask him why he gave the project a lower score on the vectors. This is a very powerful thing to know. Since Marcus is the Engineering Lead and each of the four highest-ranked projects (for this example, at least) will need a lot of input from the engineering side, his opinion holds a lot of value.

Then, you can also have other important contributing factors listed on the spreadsheet, like the level of effort the contributors scored for each project, along with their department's team sizes. If I were to look at the level of effort each project needed from engineering and the team size, then I might realize that I don't have the staff to handle four large engineering projects. Now I can make a staffing decision on top of this as well. The table below shows the Engineering, QA and UX levels of effort along with each project. You'll notice that UX has five large size projects. If they are not staffed to handle this many large size projects, then you'll have a bottleneck with UX.

I've used this model in this exact way in the past and taken that information to the CFO of the company and said, "I'm projecting a million dollars in revenue here, and the one project that is the most important to us is the project that's $240,000, one quarter of the revenue is for that. But it has a large engineering, a large QA, and a large UX size. So that is the one I would most likely cut because we don't have the resources for it." Usually, they would then ask, "What are the resources you need?" As an example, I need one designer. If we go with one designer roughly costing $10,000 a month, they would then say "I would absolutely fund one designer for $10,000 a month, knowing this project is going to deliver $240,000 per month of revenue." So now you can compare revenue to expenses and plan your resources accordingly on a roadmap like this.

ID#	Project	Eng Siz	QA Siz	UX Siz	Avg Biz Score	Biz Score Std De	ROI Biz Score	ROI Std De	Avg. Inc Rev Impact	Inc Rev St
					Business Score		ROI - Biz Score		Incremental Revenue Impact	
1	Go Together (Web view)	S	M	M	3.6	2.0	3.6	2.0	166	126
3	Recommendations data output to Fan	L	L	L	4.6	1.7	0.9	0.3	240	155
9	Shopping cart	L	L	L	2.5	1.4	0.5	0.3	172	108
16	Sell flow Improvements - Re-list ticket via apps	L	M	S	2.8	1.6	0.6	0.3	111	75
21	User generated content - pictures, videos, reviews	L	L	L	2.3	0.5	0.5	0.1	74	60
30	Native checkout (Guest checkout)	M	L	L	4.5	1.8	1.5	0.6	225	134
48	Sell Phase 2 - Pic to list	L	M	L	2.8	1.2	0.6	0.2	53	53
82	Branded FanZone - Cisco's StadiumVision	M	S	-	3.1	1.4	1.0	0.5	47	35
83	App A/B testing framework	M	M	-	3.4	1.7	1.1	0.6	217	143
87	App viral growth via user's contacts	M	M	M	2.5	1.2	0.8	0.4	72	67
91	Price Alerts without identity	L	M	-	2.7	2.2	0.5	0.4	147	119

Finally, let's say I want to see what other projects we should focus on for the quarter. Let's say that the CEO decided that conversion is all we care about, so we gave it an 80% business score weighting. If I'm deciding between two projects, one is scored 3.8 and the other 4.2 – that isn't a big difference in terms of conversion. But if I look at some of the other vectors, then the 3.8 option might come out on top. For example, let's say the project with the 3.8 score on conversion also has a net promoter score of 3.8, while the other project has a net promoter score of 1.8. It also has a big online traffic benefit, compared to the other project. The difference between the two projects' conversion scores is so slight that when I see the other benefits one project can offer compared to the other one, it might influence me to suggest going with the one that scored lower on conversion as it offers a higher overall impact across all vectors.

Here's an example of what that might look like:

ID#	Project	Contributors Conversion — Avg Conversion Score (Unweighte)	Contributors NPS — Avg NPS Score (Unweighte)	Contributors Cost Savings — Avg Cost Savings Score (Unweighte)	Contributors Traffic — Avg Traffic Score (Unweighte)	Contributors Inventory mgmt — Avg Inventory mgmt Score (Unweighte)
1	Go Together (Web view)	3.8	3.8	0.2	5.0	0.4
2	Recommendations data input from fan	0.2	0.4	0.4	0.4	0.2
3	Recommendations data output to fan	7.4	5.4	0.2	2.6	0.4
4	Optimize Android tablet layouts	1.2	1.8	0.4	0.8	0.2
5	LMS Ticket finder	0.4	1.0	0.6	0.6	0.8
6	Gift card redemption	0.8	1.4	0.8	0.6	0.2
7	One-time dismissable ""new user"" app overlay.	0.8	1.4	0.6	0.2	0.4
8	Expanded band and venue data should be	2.0	3.0	0.4	1.8	0.4
9	Shopping cart	5.0	2.2	0.6	0.4	0.8
10	Group chat / sharing prefat/post event	0.8	3.4	0.2	2.6	0.2
11	Consolidated Universal Mobile Tracking/Metrics	1.4	2.0	1.4	0.4	0.6
12	User Account preferences	0.8	1.4	0.2	0.4	0.2
13	Rewards - status and enrollment	2.2	1.8	0.6	1.4	0.8
14	Surface primary listings (e.g. AEG, MLB, Pac)	0.4	0.2	0.2	0.2	2.0
15	SH Digital Ticket - next phase - partnerships	1.2	3.0	1.0	1.2	1.2
16	Sell flow Improvements - Re-list ticket via apps	2.2	3.4	2.2	2.2	5.4
17	Enhanced map layers - heat maps for pricing	1.2	2.2	0.4	1.2	1.0
18	My Account revamp - with new gateway APIs	0.6	1.8	1.2	1.0	0.6
19	Add to user's calendar	1.0	1.2	0.8	0.8	0.2
20	Enhanced map - Social friends	1.6	3.0	0.2	1.2	0.2
21	User generated content - pictures, videos, reviews	1.2	3.0	0.2	4.2	0.2
22	Fan check-in	0.4	1.6	0.2	0.6	0.2

The flexibility of viewing your total project list with the data we've discussed above, allows you to slice and dice in any way you'd like. Below is an example of the top conversion driving projects only, but where you can also see the impact on the other vectors.

ID#	Project	Contributors Conversion	Contributors NPS	Contributors Cost Savings	Contributors Traffic	Contributors Inventory mgmt
		Avg Conversion Score (Unweighte ▼)	Avg NPS Score (Unweighte ▼)	Avg Cost Savings Score (Unweighte ▼)	Avg Traffic Score (Unweighte ▼)	Avg Inventory mgmt Score (Unweighte ▼)
1	Go Together (Web view)	3.8	3.8	0.2	5.0	0.4
3	Recommendations data output to fan	7.4	5.4	0.2	2.6	0.4
9	Shopping cart	5.0	2.2	0.6	0.4	0.8
30	Native checkout (Guest checkout)	6.6	6.2	0.6	2.2	0.8
35	Search improvements (catalog instead of LCS)	4.2	1.8	0.6	0.6	0.4
39	Create urgency for buyers	3.0	0.4	0.2	0.2	0.4
46	Location and distance	3.0	1.4	0.2	0.8	0.2
64	Native Checkout phase 3 - 1-click (PayPal API	3.2	2.0	2.8	0.2	0.2
80	Paypal incentives	3.0	1.8	2.8	1.8	0.4
83	App A/B testing framework	6.6	3.0	2.2	0.4	1.2
91	Price Alerts without idenity	3.6	3.0	0.6	2.2	0.6

Key takeaways from this chapter:

The Team Decision Matrix model allows for a great many insights into how projects or ideas can be evaluated by decision-makers. If you follow the guidance provided in this book, then you can rank and prioritize nearly any decision a product manager faces. With the combined input given by the collective team, you can gain valuable data that will help facilitate great decision making.

Chapter 3

ALWAYS KEEP CONTEXT IN MIND

Whenever I present my model to an audience, I've found that it's vital to talk about context as well. This chapter will describe for you why context is important to consider when you are using this model. It is an extremely valuable tool and does wonderful things, but can be terrible at providing value if it's not used with the correct context in mind.

Context matters a lot in business. For instance, it would be strange for a car manufacturer to start buying and selling hair products. When I'm presenting my model, I often get asked if it will work in a certain type of scenario. I've even been asked if it could be used to sort out a list of bugs for a website – the honest answer is no. Here's the thing, bugs are too small in scope to integrate well with the mechanics of my model.

Similarly, some things are just too big. You wouldn't be able to use my model to help your company decide if it should buy another company, for example. The scope of that decision is just too big with too many contributing factors to consider. My point here is, the model should be used within the right context for decisions that aren't too small and not too big for the process to be effective in its purpose.

This model of prioritization works well for steady-state products like Google Maps. What I mean is that the Team Decision Matrix model works best when it's used for adjusting already-existing projects. However, if you're planning on crafting an product from scratch, let's say that Google Maps never existed – you wouldn't be able to use this model and a spreadsheet like this, because it wasn't meant to be used like that. Creating a product from scratch involves a lot of high-impact decisions across multiple factors that cannot all be simply weighed against one another. In the future, I plan to write a book on this topic.

Always Exercise Caution

Just like context needs to always be in front of mind with the Team Decision Matrix model, caution also needs to be exercised.

You might have a high-value project that scores well across the vectors that you believe are most important. As an example, I'm going to be looking at a company who owns a magazine where the high-value project is to add user-generated content to their website. While there may be tremendous merit to the project, there's a risk that people might upload offensive material to the website. While we might think of the value of this project as being very high, there's also a downside – an aspect which we often forget to consider, especially if we're really excited about the benefits the project holds. However, if you allow people to upload whatever they want, then they just might do that, with perilous consequences for your business.

You must be thoughtful as a decision-maker to be able to make the assessment of whether you should do this project, even if the data is strongly in favor of doing it. Through this model you're simply assessing the value of an idea based on its probable impact. This model is not factoring in the probable impact of someone having malicious intent, or other potential pitfalls there are with the projects you're considering. Which is why I like to say, "Spreadsheets don't manage your business, people do." You need to have the thought process to think "what if people start uploading offensive images." One must consider more than just the data output that indicates whether something is good or profitable for the company. The Team Decision Matrix model's results should not be taken as the literal go-ahead to do something. It's a directional tool that allows you to look at a lot of options, let's say 100 projects. This is determined by how, relative to the level of investment you are prepared to make, weighed against their impact on vectors of company value as assessed by the people closest to the product. Then you can easily see which ones are the highest value.

Once you have the data, you can see what level of agreement you have based on the standard deviation within these top 10 options. If our most important vector is conversion, then I can see which of them score the best on conversion? I'll find one in the list and then look at the other vectors and factors like time management. Maybe I see that it has a large engineering size, so then I'd want to look at the ones that have the highest impact and the lowest engineering expense. I'd narrow it down to one or two projects. This model allows me to get to a smaller list to choose from, instead of the full list of 100 options – which might have led to indecision paralysis. But what it doesn't do is take the broader situation or the potential risks into context. That part is still entirely up to those making the decisions.

You can't let a spreadsheet decide everything for you. But this is a tool that helps you narrow down the number of things that you need to think about or consider, and you can then decide amongst fewer options.

There is one more thing to mention regarding caution. I have seen in the past that this process can make people become a little territorial. There have been instances where one person may feel like they have an outsized voice in the decision-making process of the feature list. I've heard someone say, "If I and my other business counterpart are only two of twelve people voting on projects in this spreadsheet then there's no way we're ever going to win because we only have two of twelve votes." I then replied that if they're starting off with the perspective that they need a 51% authority against this decision, then this will never work, regardless of what process we use. From a potential pitfall perspective, if people are walking into your meeting with this type of negative spirit, then you have the wrong alignment at an intellectual level with your peers.

Key takeaways from this chapter:

It's important to always keep the context in mind when choosing new projects because a spreadsheet won't be able to do that for you. The spreadsheet is very helpful when it comes to narrowing down your options and making a calculated decision, but it cannot decide everything for you, and it also won't help you see any potential downsides to a decision. You need to look at the broader picture and consider all the variables that cannot be put into a spreadsheet.

Chapter 4

OTHER USES OF PRIORITIZATION AND RANK MODEL

This exact model can be used to prioritize other types of decisions. All you need to do is change the vectors and features you put in. Let's look at how the Team Decision Matrix model can affect the decision-making process in other departments, like talent performance reviews or candidate assessment.

Business Score Weighting	
Data-driven	35%
Conflict management	25%
Teamwork	5%
Presentation skills	25%
Intellectual horsepower	10%
	100%

Here's the vector part of the spreadsheet again, and this time the company goal vectors like conversion and traffic were replaced with new attributes like data-driven and teamwork.

The process of giving weight scores to each vector is repeated, and you simply replace the project names and descriptions with people's names.

	Data-driven	Conflict management	Teamwork	Presentation skills	Intellectual horsepower
Lauren	L	-	M	S	L
Jeff	S	L	-	L	M
Jaclyn	M	M	S	-	M
Danika	S	M	S	-	S
Stuart	-	M	-	S	-
Ryan	M	M	S	-	-
Eniola	-	L	-	M	-
Jose	M	M	S	-	S
Hilary	S	M	-	-	-
Jennifer	M	M	S	M	-
John	L	M	S	-	M
Chris	M	M	S	-	M
Tommy	S	M	S	-	S

After that, you can get the right team leaders to give an assessment on each person. The data you've gathered using this process can be used in many ways, including determining which person deserves a promotion and who should be hired for a new position. Or you could even have a specific vector that you're focusing on because you want to see who has the best teamwork skills. The possibilities with this model are vast and can be applied to many different company departments.

Now let's move away from the business environment to a more personal setting. I'm proud of the fact that you can rank and prioritize nearly anything with this model - even in a personal context. Let's imagine that you're planning a vacation and you have a few places that you're considering. There are many possible vectors to choose from here, depending on your specific vacation needs, but for this example's sake, we can look at vectors like relaxation, historical significance, total cost, distance from home, and duration of stay.

When scoring these value vectors one can mathematically calculate the value of each vacation option. Then when indicating the weighted average for each vector, you can ensure that what you value most has a higher rating. For example, suppose your kids are of the age where exposing them to something historical is meaningful. You can place a weighted average value of 40% on historical significance, whereas the other attributes each get a portion of the remaining 60%. Then, when you score the Small, Medium, Large or No impact for each vacation option, the result is likely a prioritized list of vacation destinations based on what is important to you or your family's needs.

That was just one quick example of how the Team Decision Matrix model can be used to make decisions in your personal life. Of course, this isn't applicable to every situation, and not every decision can be made by simply putting in some data on a list. Which is why I highlighted the need for context and caution in the previous chapter. When it comes to making personal decisions, a spreadsheet like this can be very helpful, but it shouldn't be the only deciding factor for making a decision. Instead, it can help you narrow down your choices so that you don't become overwhelmed by them. Let's take choosing a new car as an example. That's usually one of the toughest choices to make because there are so many options out there. However, if you prioritize well and know what features you value more in a car, then the process doesn't have to be a big headache.

Some vectors you might choose when deciding on a new car:

Business Score Weighting	
Vehicle ergonomics	35%
Trunk space	25%
Safety	5%
Fuel consumption	25%
Modern technology	10%
	100%

After that, you can list all the vehicles you've been considering or, even all the vehicles within a certain price range, if that's a very big determining factor for you. Then, you can approach the assessment phase by either doing research on your own and assessing each car yourself, or you could approach dealerships/friends who knows a lot about cars, and ask them to assess each car model.

In the end, you might be left with a few options that are the most suited to your needs. At least, relative to the options you've chosen to list, since this model is only as good as the data you put into it. Now that you have fewer options to choose from, you can really get down to the details of these top vehicles on your list and see which one you like the most. Each vehicle will fulfill the needs you've outlined through the vectors you've chosen, but the ultimate choice will still be yours.

Key takeaways from this chapter:

The Team Decision Matrix model can be used in many different business and social contexts. While it has been developed with product management in mind, its core principles are applicable across a broader spectrum. So, whenever you have a tough decision to make that has a lot of options to choose from, consider using this model to narrow down your choices so that when the time comes to decide, you won't feel overwhelmed.

Conclusion

I've actively used this model myself for about five years now and delivered multiple presentations about it to crowds of people. What this model did during my time at StubHub was increase their overall metrics by three times. When I joined StubHub, the mobile app conversion rate was about 3%. Which means, three out of every 100 people who visited the StubHub mobile app would transact with a ticket. The conversion rate was at around 12% when I left. I heard that StubHub is still using this model as of the time of this book's publishing and that their conversion rate is even higher than

12%. All of that was achieved on the back of decisions made while using this process.

I've also seen staff tenure go up at one of the companies where I've implemented this model. Why did it have this type of effect? Because it reduces the impact that personality and title can have on decision-making. The Team Decision Matrix model neutralizes the effect of personal influence on the decision-making process. How many times, if you're in the product management or decision-making capacity, have you asked engineers what direction they think the team should take? That probably doesn't happen very often. Because you're the leader, right, you have the title that says you can tell them what to do. But I don't believe in that. I want the opinions of the team. When we start asking people what they think you should do, there's a couple of great dynamics that come out of that:

- The first and most important: they are invested in what's happening. They are invested in the success of that project because they had a hand in choosing it and making decisions around it. It wasn't dictated to them. They said that they believe in doing this and their manager agreed, so now they're on the hook for it. They now have a reason to be invested in the success of it. That doesn't show up on a spreadsheet or in revenue. It shows up in retention.

- Retention happens because employees feel valued and know that their opinions matter. If you can lengthen the amount of time people stay with your company, it can have a tremendous impact on all your economics, like cost structure and customer satisfaction. Everything benefits when you're focusing on your people.

- Think about the people you interact with every day - we're a very diverse population. People come from different educational backgrounds, different ethnicities, different languages. When you get people together in a room to start making decisions, you're going to get people who are shy, some who are outspoken, some who just joined the company and don't know as much as the others, and there's also the title (HiPPO) thing going on in the room. All those things are neutralized when you get to data. That's the real core of the Team Decision Matrix model: data tells all.

People tend to respect this approach because it brings transparency and data to a process that often didn't have it. Whereas if you have a person who's just simply deciding things and telling everyone what they're going to do next, then you're in a vacuum where people question those decisions and wonder, "What data do you have to inform that decision?" Or, "why should we do that?" That person could be making the decision based on who they spoke to last or on the word of the CEO who told them what to do next. Their peers know this person is deciding on something like a feature without knowing the cost. It's basically not being thorough when accumulating data to build a summary and make an informed decision. This isn't helpful to productivity or potential project success.

What it all comes down to is a balancing act. You have this vision and you aspire to do great things. However, there are loud and opinionated voices. How do you bring data into the equation and empower your people? If you're really focused and thoughtful about how to move an entire division of people forward, then the tools and mechanisms here, around setting a vision, deciding projects, and empowering people, will help you do so. It certainly has helped me.